IT'S EASY TO BE LOVED

(ALL YOU HAVE TO BE IS LOVABLE.)

POEMS BY WILLIAM HARGER

WITH PHOTOGRAPHS BY RON SUGIYAMA
AND WILLIAM HARGER

Celestial Arts
Millbrae, Ca 94030

First Printing, June 1974
Library of Congress Card No.: 74-8286
ISBN 0-912310-56-1
Made in the United States of America

Today is such a fine day.
Hope is in the air,
birds are dashing here and there,
and the frost-lace
on the window
frames my view of mountains
greening their hello
to my awakening.
I think
I'll just spend the entire day
flying in place.

I once knew this lady. . . . .
This god-awful beautiful lady.
She was one of those ladies
everybody wanted
and needed
and, of course
she just could never
have enough time
for all of them.
You know how it is. . . . .
you've seen them.
A magnificent
aware
in front of it all lady
and
she told me she loved me.
I couldn't believe it.
I couldn't believe I could be
so important
to someone as important as she.
I couldn't believe
she could love me!
And I remember well
her first undress
in my full view.
She was flawless
and the combination
of what I knew
her thoughts for me to be,
and her wondrous
flashing form,
moving towards me,
to be given,
was greatly more than I could bear.
It was the most religious experience
I ever had.
She was God.

Birds of a feather
fluck
together

What is love?

My grandmother says
it's just a funny word
made up by man
because he doesn't understand
his feelings.

I love her.

One thing I might still enjoy
is falling as I did
as a boy
for a lady.
I don't know why
I haven't tried that lately.
I don't know why
I haven't felt the warmth
tingle over me
at some first touch
and
I don't know why
I haven't seen those dreams
flashing by the inside of my eyes much
and I don't know why
I haven't realized
any of those old loving schemes lately.
Oh,
just once again,
before I become to old a man
to perform the promises
lovers promise one another .....
just one more time
I might still enjoy
falling for a lady
and feel my feelings welling up
inside my chest
as I mistakenly touch her breast
with innocent,
wandering fingers
she wouldn't detest
for being clumsy.
Yes,
one thing I might still enjoy
is the supreme joy I felt,
as a boy,
when falling for a lady.

I'm a racehorse;
highly tuned,
spirited
with no more flesh upon my bones
than my design
should carry with me.
I'm a racehorse;
straining at the gate,
wanting out,
and swiftly dancing 'round the track
enclosed in shout
and swear
and hankies flashing in the air.
I'm a racehorse;
different than all the rest,
made for something more
than pulling plows
or plodding into the timberline
with some fat lady
on my spine
groaning all the time.
I'm a racehorse;
fleet of foot
and swift of mind
and my muscled sheen in a pastured sun
is almost more than anyone
could bear to see
without wondering wistfully
why they couldn't be
a racehorse just like me
But,
I am not the only horse
composed as I'm. . . . .
there are many other horses too
that can do most everything
I can do
and I must accept in my wondrous mind
that even in their perfect prime
racehorses do not win
everytime.
But I'm a racehorse
And I'm beautiful.

There was once
a flower
blooming
in the wild, free forest
of my youth.
A flower of hue and grace
and such promise
that I was justly put
to nourish
and be most attentive
to the place in which
this flower shined its lovely face.
But,
though most flowers survive
each ordeal of their season,
my flower wilted
premature
and all the care
which I did endeavour
at its slender stem
could not revive my flower
from its downhill trend
and she died,
without any reasons I could see,
whatever.
And,
to this day
I'm not enlightened yet
except
I've learned I must accept
the dying of the flowers
and I must leave the dead flowers lay.

A brisk force
is sucking at my mind. . . . .
pulling at it
to feel
and scream
and know
the joy of nothing.

Sometimes,
when the wind blows,
I stand at the window
and watch the tops of trees
and the surface of the water
and the blossoms,
swirling,
and the birds
and the leaves,
flashing,
and I try to think of something
important
but I never can.
Besides that,
I think I just missed the point.

I don't look the same
to my friends
anymore
because they're not my friends
anymore.

I like girls
because
they have things the world needs,
badly,
and I can get them,
if I need them,
when I go to them.
Girls have things like
softness,
warmth,
forthrightness,
honesty,
compassion,
protectiveness,
and strength.
That's why I like girls.
And,
the only time I like a man
is when he's like that.

It's easy to be loved.
All you have to be
is
lovable.

I find God
everywhere I look these days.
I find God
in breezes
and cock-a-doodle-doos.
I find God
in children
and sand bars
and deserts
and in the shoes of some old man
shuffling along the sidewalk.
Yes,
I find God
everywhere I look these days
and I found him
all by myself.

With love
does not come peace
and glory.
With love
does not come calm
and warmth
and timeless times.
With love
does not come brotherhood
and strength
and pride.
No,
with love
does not come these.
Comes instead
turmoil for peace,
fear for glory;
fervor and pounding heart beats
for calm;
suspicion for warmth;
and cheap,
fleeting,
cramped minutes,
for timeless times;
separation,
jealousy
even battle for brotherhood;
sneakiness for strength;
and excuses for pride.
Yes,
love comes not
with that we would have
but
love comes. . . . .
love comes.

I don't really want to go to bed
but I've got nothing to do
that might take the place
of my playing dead
for a few hours.

The folly of my life
isn't that
I've given nothing
and offered nothing
or aided nothing.
The folly of my life
isn't that
I've created little
or shared little
or loved little.
No. . . .
these were not my failures
and my follies.
My folly
was worrying
about the things
you thought of me. . . .
as though you
were more important!

The young dog
sniffed the old dog
and the old dog
growled,
low,
deep down in this chest.

The young dog
waited a while
and then he licked the old dog's fur
and the old dog
snarled
and curled his lip.

The young dog
waited a day or so,
then
he touched noses with the old dog
and the old dog
barked
and snapped.

The young dog
waited a time longer
and then
he barked,
playfully,
and wagged his tail,
wildly,
with his rear in the air
and his chest on the ground
and his dancing paws in front of him
and the old dog
bit him on the nose,
hard.
So,
the young dog ate him.

God, God—
You've done it again. . .
Another day for me!

I started out alone
and
I ended up alone.
It's funny. . . . .
that everything in between,
that meant so much,
meant so little.

I was thinking about you
the other night.
Nothing special. . . .
just thinking about you.
I poured myself a drink,
lit a fire,
and sat there,
in the dark,
thinking about you.
You have good breath.
You know,
I thought about how
I love to place my nose
as close to your mouth
as I can
to inhale your words
as well
as hear them.
And,
I thought about your slim legs,
and hip bones,
and good rounds.
Yeah,
I stared off into the dark
the other night
and thought about you
and wanted you.

In my mind
I've often heard it said,
"there's no such thing
as love."
I heard in there
that people speaking of love
have not the slightest notion
of what they're really speaking of.
I heard
it's just a silly game
we had to give a name to
because
so many people play it.
I heard,
when we say it,
we're really only opening a door
to something else
not love at all.
And yet,
deep down in my stomach,
way inside my gut,
exists a rumbling feeling for you
that should I give it,
and should you let me,
love might yet infect me
and I might come to love you.

You ask me
how much I love you?
Well,
I love you blue tones
and soft, pumping surges
deep in my stomach,
and I love you frenzied red
with fringes of flashes
of butterfly wings
and witch doctor's bones.
I love you a flower
with eleven white petals
'round a single orange eye
high on a stem
surrounded by grass.
You ask me how much I love you. . . . .?
I love you
with all of my ass.

Being free
is like
being on a pendulum
that's swinging out
and
isn't ever coming back.

The peach hue
of your face
glowing against the light
is quite a sight to see.
It taunts me
to touch you at your cheek,
your lips,
with fingertips
which never will be used
so perfectly
because I'm afraid.
Oh,
to have the right
to touch your delicate face,
lock you in a fine embrace,
and carry you to some private place
where I might tell you
of my love
in more explicit ways
than sitting here at couch-length,
afraid,
and smiling politely.

My love for you
is not
a common love
for
common love
is not love at all
to me.
My love for you
is Indian
and Irish
and rushing leaves
along soft roads
and
my love for you
is not new. . . . .
it's old.

I had a girl once
who'd take my head
and set in her lap
and begin to ramble
thru my hair
and in my ears
and 'cross my lips
along my brows and down my nose
and softly on my chest
in her sweet way
to settle my mood
and tear my mind from care
and I am sure
to drift me into sleep
as I lay softly in her lap.
She was a dear girl
but I could never go to sleep. . . . . .
there.

A man met life
walking down the road
and asked:
"Why was life
such a heavy load to carry.
And why should I even try. . . .
why?"
And life replied:
"It's not for me
to try to be your answer,
my friend.
It's not for me
to be your whys or when.
'Tis only for me
to pass on by."
And life slipped on,
leaving the man behind.

A child met life
on the road
the next day.
The child said:
"Hi,"
and skipped on by.
Life smiled
and paused a tiny while,
giving the child
all the time he needed.

Promises
stop things from moving on.

As I drew you from the couch
where you just lay
I knew I'd not find you again.
I knew we didn't feel the things together
once we felt.
And,
I knew the door
would be my good-bye to you.

Oh,
to have the fine full love
once we felt.
To have again
the wandering Autumns
and our bag of wine
and the good touches
beneath some round tree,
high,
in the mountains of our dreams.
To share again
the friends together
we shared together then
and to share the love
we felt there-in.

Yes,
as I drew you from the couch,
I knew the door
would be my good-bye.

I loved you,
you know,
I loved you.

When you're in pain,
try laughing.
When you're in trouble,
smile,
turn your back,
and dance away.
When you're pressed by things
just beyond your understanding
and they've already
begun to hurt,
wade in,
swinging,
taking deep breaths
and singing your praises to the opposition.
When you're hurting,
wince,
but find a lap
to place your head upon for strokes
and gentle kisses.
Yeah, when it's bad in any way
say
"I don't give a damn!
I am what I am!
And I won't let you people put me down!"
Try these things
In pressing times
and find. . . . . .
nothing works!
When you're down you're down
and
nothing works!

You enrage me world
with your promises of better things to come.
You enrage me with your simple faith.
World,
can't you see
in the collected lies of history
that we won't do a thing
to make things better. . . . .
only worse?
Can't you see
world
you must crumble—
you must tumble in the end
by all the things mankind will bring you?
Can't you see
we're playing games
of killing all we can of you?
Won't you strike us back?
Won't you put a stop
to what we're doing
to your inner workings,
to your organs,
to your soul?
Won't you strike us back
and end your senseless waiting
while my kind is calculating
how to hurt you more
or
are you to continue,
softly waiting in your glow of sun,
beautiful,
and perhaps dying. . . . .
perhaps done.

In the still of the night
I remember
times
with you.
I don't know anymore
why I don't know where you are
anymore.
I was certain
before
I would never lose touch. . . .
I would always have you
when I wanted you
because
it was sure to be what you wanted too.
But I don't even know
where you are anymore.
Distance has swallowed you
and time has made you
invisible
and all our promises
have become memories
dying
some remorseless death.
Funny,
once you were everything
to me.

Down in the city,
when I was a boy,
when you could still see the stars
at night,
when you were still allowed
out-of-doors after dark,
and when you had no fear
of being out there alone,
with my dog,
when dogs were still allowed to roam
without leashes,
and with my girl friend,
before I knew she was a girl,
or at least before I knew what girls
were for,
on the sidewalk,
still warm from the sun
that still shined clearly then,
we used to lie on our backs,
my girl and I,
dog in between,
and watch the sky twinkle and gleam
when I was young.

One thing I've learned. . . . .
the world will be okay without me.
As okay
as it would have been,
that is,
had I not come to be.
I guess I knew even before I got started
I would never see success.
I guess I knew it would be fruitless.
But,
something in me,
something far too deep
for me to understand
or for anybody else to see,
if they should find the time to—
something in me
bade that I should try.
Something better than I had ever been.
Well,
we didn't win,
that thing and I,
but much better do I feel
that we took the time
to try.
It's all done now
and even though no one else got the message,
I've found I believe what I've been saying,
and I'm in a softer
and warmer
place.

Into the blue eye
of a summer day
he spread his little wings
and sailed away.
Into the blue eye
of a summer day
he pranced on tiny feet
to greet
a stone perhaps,
or perhaps some weedy thing
or any else
his day could bring.
Ah,
to be a child again
and delve in childlike things
without fear—
without fear.

I was sitting in a large room
watching people
watching people
as people do
and my eyes fell upon a fellow
seemingly enveloped
in a pale of gloom.
He was staring at the fire,
in the fireplace burning,
and the look on his face
was yearning for the face
he saw there. . . .
      sparks for eyes,
      flames for hair,
      distorted air for curves and thighs,
and as he watched
I realized
I had become consumed
by the flames consuming him
and I joined him in his whim
and wanted her too!

Love is a rare
message.
To give it one must
have received a pulse
from warm nights
and skipping days.
To receive it one must
know truth
and softness
and one must have hungered
for the warmth
and time
and timeless times
and the flesh of his
or her
lover.
Love is a rare message.
To give it one must
understand smells
and light
and dying, dreadful nights
and to receive it
one must live in despair
once or twice.
But
to love is a nice thing,
at any cost.

I awoke this day
to a diamond.
I couldn't believe
God still turns 'em
out like this
after all we've done
to the air.

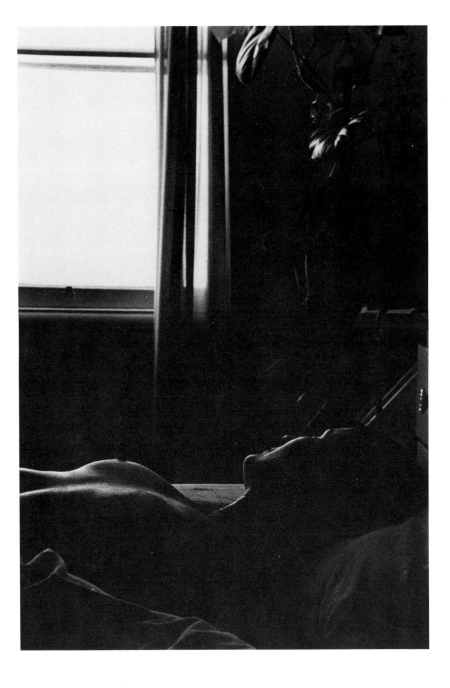

I'm being called
by a cleanliness
I've not felt
or heard
before.
Soon,
I will understand.
Soon,
I will die
into new life.
You will not know me
anymore
but,
soon,
I will breathe again.

• INDEX •